Classical Education

&

The Home School

| DOUGLAS | WESLEY | DOUGLAS |
| WILSON | CALLIHAN | JONES |

Canon Press
MOSCOW, IDAHO

Douglas Wilson, Wesley Callihan, and Douglas Jones, *Classical Education and the Home School*

© 1995 by Canon Press, P.O. Box 8741, Moscow, ID 83843

ISBN: 1-885767-08-0

Contents

Introduction

As we survey the educational ruins around us, classical and Christian education appears to be an idea whose time has come. Actually, in the light of history, it is a concept whose time has come *again*. More and more Christian parents are seeing the failures of modern socialistic education—and these failures have been monumental—such parents are hungering for a *substantive* alternative, one that has been tested before, and found to be good. Classical and Christian education presents them with just such an alternative.

Parents are coming to see that it is not enough simply to pull the kids out of the government schools. When a demon is cast out, and nothing put in its place, the final result can be seven times worse (Matt. 12:45). Reactionary Christian education is consequently not really a permanent alternative. Many Christian parents who had initially just reacted to the godlessness of the government schools are now seeing the shallowness of that kind of Christian response. They have become hungry, on behalf of their children, for an education that is unabashedly Christian, rigorous, and thorough. At the same time, parents who think this way also commonly acknowledge they really do not fully understand what it is they desire.

This brief treatment aims to present some of the basic principles and methods of a classical and Christian education, tailored for use in a homeschool setting. One of the primary purposes of classical education is to equip the students to learn for themselves. So, in a similar way, the purpose of this booklet is to set interested parents on this path and to give them some of the basic information they will need to walk through it. Even though it is an unfamiliar path to many of us, it is still well-worn from centuries of use, and it should be possible for us to feel at home there once again.

At the same time, we should remember that a classical and Christian education is not a "package deal." No one supplier or textbook publisher will provide you with everything you need in a fifty-pound box, delivered by UPS. Western culture weighs more than this, and the abandonment of the fast-food, convenience-store mentality which currently surrounds education is one of the first indications that we are making significant progress.

In a very real sense, this kind of classical education results in a certain mindset, a certain orientation. It is that mindset which is briefly set forth and commended in this small booklet. Parents who undertake this pattern for education will, of necessity, feel very alone in some respects. But as the process continues, they will make many friends— some living and walking the same path with them, and many others dead and pleasantly entombed in their favorite books.

So what is presented here is nothing more than amiable company for the first few steps on these "older paths" and a rough, sketched-out map for the remainder of the journey. *Deus vobiscum.*

The Classical Bias Toward Language

When we speak of a classical education, we speak, in part, of that education common to older Britain and transplanted into early America. The classical English emphasis on a mastery of language disciplines, especially Latin and rhetoric, helped ground generations of superior leaders and thinkers.

Traditionally, a classical education began either in the home or a local grammar school, and, for some, continued through into its depths in the college years. That great Puritan thinker Cotton Mather summarized early Harvard's basic requirements for incoming students. Notice the striking contrast of expectations between the grammar schools of yesteryear and those of our own day:

> When scholars had so far profited at the *grammar schools*, that they could read any *classical author* into English, and readily make and speak true *Latin*, and write it in *verse* as well as *prose*; and perfectly decline the *paradigms* of *nouns* and *verbs* in the Greek tongue, they were judged capable of admission in *Harvard College.*[1]

Similarly, early Yale required,

> That none may expect to be admitted into this College unless upon examination of the President and Tutors, they shall be found able extempore to read, construe, and parce Tully, Virgil, and the Greek Testament: and to write true Latin prose and to understand the Rules of Prosodia, and com-

---

[1] Cited in Richard Hofstadter,ed., *American Higher Education* Vol. 1 (Chicago: Univ. of Chicago Press, 1961) p. 17.

mon arithmetic, and shall bring sufficient testimony of his blameless and inoffensive life.[2]

Most other colleges expected similar classical training as the
basis for a student *starting* work in higher education. But
these early schools expected not just proficiency in languages,
they also expected students to study within an explicitly
Christian framework to the glory of God. For the devout, a
secular classical education was a contradiction in terms. Take
for example the stated purposes of early William and Mary
College of 1727. Note below how the statement naturally
combines classical and Christian (Protestant) aspects in its
purposes:

> Toward the cultivating the minds of men, and rec-
> tifying their manners, what a mighty influence the
> studies of good letters, and the liberal sciences
> have, appears from hence, that these studies not
> only flourished of old amongst those famous na-
> tions, the Hebrews, Egyptians, Greeks, and Ro-
> mans; but in the latter ages of the world likewise,
> after a great interruption and almost destruction
> of them, through the incursions of the barbarous
> nations, they are at last retrieved, and set up with
> honor in all considerable nations. Upon this there
> followed the reformation of many errors and
> abuses in the point of religion, and the institution
> of youth to the duties of Christian virtues and
> civility; and a due preparation of fit persons for
> all offices in church and state.[3]

The early Harvard statutes similarly declare that "everyone
shall consider the main end of his life and studies, to know

---

[2] *Ibid.* p. 54.
[3] *Ibid.* p. 39.

God and Jesus Christ which is Eternal life—John 17.3."[4] Obviously, these early colleges have long since betrayed their original purposes in regard to both classical and Christian education. Nonetheless, in their godly prime, they left us many influential Christian leaders, thinkers, and citizens.

Homeschoolers drawn to instilling a classical education similar in rigor to the early grammar schools must note that such training did not succeed simply by adding Latin or Greek or rhetoric to a typical curriculum. A genuinely classical education developed a particular kind of disciplined heart and mind. It required a certain cultural mold. It assumed an environment bursting with language, in stark contrast to our own more image-centered day. The classical and Christian mind was a mind surrounded by an ocean of *language*. Every day, all day, in family devotions, work, education, recreation, church, and civil duties—language, as opposed to communication by images, governed experience. Such a bias toward language, typical especially of the Puritans, naturally produced minds and habits very different from those of a culture like our own.

First, consider some of the demands of language on our hearts and minds. We so often miss the strange beauty of language. For example, we communicate with symbols and sounds that don't resemble the items they represent. The words "dog" and "car," for example, do not resemble any dogs or cars in our neighborhood. And somehow, when we arrange these squiggly black marks (d, o, g) on this page, a reader thousands of miles away can do some bizarre thing called "understanding" in which the symbols are translated into thoughts and somehow our minds link, even when the original author has long gone on to think about something else. The entire process of communicating and understand-

---

[4] *Ibid.* p. 8.

ing is so wildly complex that we are still just scratching our heads to try and figure out all that is involved. And yet, by the grace of God, tiny children almost miraculously master so much in so little time.

In addition to language's almost supernatural strangeness, it also requires very precise mental disciplines. Other forms of communication, like pictures and photographs, require altogether different habits of mind. One observer, Neil Postman, gives a short example of the disciplines involved in reading:

> You are required, first of all, to remain more or less immobile for a fairly long time. . . . You must also have learned to pay no attention to the shapes of the letters on the page. You must see through them, so to speak, so that you can go directly to the meanings they form. . . . At the same time you must be able to tell from the tone of the language what is the author's attitude toward the subject and toward the reader. In judging the quality of an argument, you must be able to do several things at once, including delaying a verdict until the entire argument is finished, holding in mind questions until you have determined where, when or if the text answers them. . . . You must be able to withhold those parts of your knowledge and experience, which, in fact, do not have a bearing on the argument. And in preparing to do all of this, you must have learned to negotiate the world of abstractions, for there are very few phrases and sentences in this book that require you to call forth concrete images. In print culture, we are apt to say of people who are not intelligent that we must "draw them pictures" so that they may understand.

Intelligence implies that one can dwell comfortably without pictures, in a field of concepts and generalizations.[5]

In contrast to the demands of reading, Postman and others have noted that observing pictures involves different habits. Pictures are judged more in terms of their effect on our senses and emotions, especially the eyes. We generally judge pictures in terms of their beauty or ugliness and cannot judge them true or false like an assertion of language. Pictures have no premises or conclusions, and children don't need to struggle through years of phonics training to grasp a basic picture, but they do to grasp a basic sentence. Moreover, representative pictures, like photographs and icons, can only give us images of specific things. Whereas language symbols, whether in regular reading or arithmetic or music, instantly force our thinking into the world of types, kinds, abstractions, and generalizations, a world that can't be depicted by photographs.

Apart from the ancient pagan devotion to images and statues, the classical world could not readily drown itself in images from billboards, colorful newsmagazines, television flickerings, and neon shopping malls. It had to develop its culture and institutions primarily in the medium of language. And given the mental disciplines demanded by reading and conversation, they developed the strength of mind so absent from our modern cultures. To us, the early entrance requirements into Harvard and Yale may seem overwhelming, but to many children of the time (not all) who had been steeped in language and its demands every day since birth, the expectations were within reach.

We are so distant from that former world of language

---

[5] *Amusing Ourselves to Death* (New York: Penguin Books, 1984), p. 25.

that we might find it hard to imagine living in a place so rarely dotted with pictorial representations. Given the natural habits and disciplines required by language, we shouldn't be surprised that those cultures which embraced the heightened demands of classical education should have excelled so well in literature, music, mathematics, and leadership in both church and state. We must work for the same for our children.

This classical bias in favor of the linguistic over pictorial communication finds its grounding in Scripture. There we discover that God Himself chose to reveal Himself primarily through this odd medium of language. And instead of allowing His people to worship Him via images like the other nations, God strictly prohibited them from thinking of Him in terms of pictures. Edward Veith notes that Scripture repeatedly shows its bias against overemphasizing the visual:

> Notice that the Bible never describes what Jesus or anyone else looked like. Nor are there extended spatial descriptions of "background," the leisurely description of setting and atmosphere taken for granted in Western literature. Homer, by contrast, is full of the most vivid visual descriptions—"the white-armed Hera," the red-gold hair of Achilles, the exhaustively detailed picture of his immortal shield. . . . For the Hebrews, one related conceptually to other people not by seeing them but by hearing them. Thus, to take an important example, there is little talk of *seeing* God in the Bible. Such an experience is reserved for the future life . . . . God's *Word* is the basis for relationship with Him.[6]

---

[6] Gene Veith, *State of the Arts* (Wheaton, IL: Crossway Books, 1991, pp. 158,159).

In the New Testament, the supreme revelation of God is described as the "Word." And the Lord even summarizes day to day Christian living by minimizing the place of the visual: "For our light affliction, which is but for a moment, is working for us a far more exceeding and eternal weight of glory, while we do not look at the things which are seen, but at the things which are not seen. For the things which are seen are temporary, but the things which are not seen are eternal" (2 Cor. 6:17,18).

If the medium of communication and education were completely unimportant, then such emphases would not matter at all. But God Himself directs our biases down particular paths. Our educational method ought to be informed by such insights as well.

Given the classical and Christian bias toward language, we can recognize several insights for instilling a classical education via the home school.

First, such a bias toward language is not easy to reproduce, but it is central to a classical education. To begin with, we don't acquire any of our habits in brief spurts of practice. We acquire our habits best when we live in an environment biased toward strengthening those habits. Home schoolers can be uniquely advantaged in this aspect of classical education. They can provide a constant environment which holds forth the primacy of language in every area of life. They can fill their homes and lives with a devotion and ongoing interest in the issues of language, literature, and rich conversation. Some of us even explicitly minimize the use of pictorial communication ("Picture books are for babies") and magnify the beauties and subtleties of written and spoken communication.

Most home schoolers have an obvious aversion to popular television, but by regularly providing their children with "decent" cartoons and video games, they do nothing to encourage the habits of reading . Linguistic symbols and pictorial representations encourage entirely different habits of mind. For some of us, not all, this suggests that we might tell our young ones that they may watch an excellent movie when they are young adults, when their minds have been more firmly molded to the disciplines of reading. By then, though, they will probably not be able to bear much of the inherent shallowness of even the best cinema when compared to the riches of Austen, Dickens, Bronte, and Dostoyevsky. But everything has its place, even relatively mindless activities.

Such comments do not imply a legalistic or strict Ludditism against any use of pictures or video, but rather as an exhortation for developing good classical habits. Whatever the division of time between pictures and language, language should far crowd out anything else. Pictures, photography, and excellent art, of course, have their important places, but they cannot *dominate* or even have a significant place in an education if we want to nurture a disciplined classical mind in our children.

Second, the classical emphasis on language training should at least give us pause when considering the wide host of educational subjects available. Homeschoolers are often pressured to include every subject under the sun—geography, science, history, social studies, on and on. Resist the pressure. These things have their place, but in early America, the grammar schools focused primarily on mastering the language disciplines and gained most of their history, for example, by reading Scripture and the classical authors. Parents should aim first to create masters of language in writing, reading, and speaking, and then they can involve the other objects.

The classical skills of language involve more than just English and Latin studies. Arithmetic, for example, involves linguistic symbols as well. Like "regular" reading, it requires learning to interpret, memorize, understand mathematical grammar, and work with abstractions. One advantage of teaching and learning arithmetic is that it has none of those pesky "irregular" words or violations of its basic grammar. The rules entirely lack exceptions!

A classical appreciation of arithmetic should also give us a healthy skepticism about new claims and fads. When something new shows up in the latest homeschool catalogues, we should ask how a classical instructor three or even fifteen hundred years ago would have dealt with this item. For example, the vast array of colorful mathematics rods and manipulables have now taken a place of established orthodoxy in many quarters. Some insist that we can't teach mathematics properly without constant manipulables. But how did past students do so well before Cuisenaire came along? We should be more skeptical. Moreover, like other language disciplines, arithmetic and especially counting are a beautifully abstract and rich aspect of God's creation. Abstract thinking is crucial and not evil, despite the modern urge to make everything, including arithmetic, concrete. Both the abstract (the general) and the concrete (the specific) have their places in God's creation. We need to force ourselves into a more classical mindset to evaluate new claims.

One final point may help when assembling a classical curriculum. A focus on language disciplines, including Latin and arithmetic, should open our eyes to the importance of living foreign languages as well. We've all probably heard how students in Europe regularly and almost effortlessly speak at least two but commonly three or four contemporary languages. French and German had long been a mainstay of English education. Of course, the Europeans have very practical reasons to pick up other languages, being so close to different language groups. But we too can greatly benefit from other living languages. They not only encourage more of the classical emphasis on language disciplines, they also open wide new worlds in literature and life for us.

Small children often take gleeful delight in speaking in a foreign tongue and gobble it up. Parents might also choose a language or two that draws on family roots of some sort or one that has prominence in your community (Spanish, in the Southwest, for example).

The drawback to including living languages is, of course, that most American parents lack fluency of their own. But this is no excuse. With the explosion of homeschooling materials now available, many fine foreign-language programs for children surround us. Search out the local library if cost is prohibitive. Parents themselves may take a course at a local college, if need be. At some point, some parents, if they are able, might want to hire a student from a local college to come to tutor in their home. If parents make foreign language a priority, they can find some means to satisfy that goal.

Third, resist the overpowering temptation to make education entertaining. As always, entertainment has its place, but we live in an era that seeks to make everything giddy. Politics, music, news, work, phonics, and even worship before a holy God has to be funny before Moderns will embrace it. Just say no. We've often bought the modern lie that children will only learn if the subject is fun and thrilling. But self-discipline is rarely entertaining; it should involve hard work and sweat. Education is a discipline. So much education about God's commands and world requires sustained, careful, even painful study, that we really rob our children if we allow them to expect cheap entertainment in education. Train your children to oppose the urge to make everything fun. Surround them with family proverbs such as "the best things in life take hard work." Explain to them how creation is divided up so that some things call for fun, others for calm meditation, and still others for the utmost reverence. "To everything there is a season. . . . A time to kill, and a time to heal; a time to break down, and a time to build up; a time to weep, and a time to laugh; a time to mourn, and a time to dance; . . . . a time to keep silence, and a time to speak; a time to love, and a time to hate" (Eccl. 3:1ff.). Moderns collapse God's beautiful array of life into one constant dull response: entertainment, entertainment, entertainment. A classical and Christian perspective in education gives us a reprieve from such frenzy. It reminds us to slow down, to read carefully, to meditate calmly, to work honorably. It shouldn't be easy.

The Necessity of Hard Work

To give to someone else what one never received one's self is, of course, difficult. Many parents are initially attracted to the idea of a classical education because they know that they were shortchanged in their own education; they want their children to be taught in a way that they were not. The problem with this is a problem common in all forms of conversion, including academic conversions—one is turning away from the familiar to embrace the unfamiliar. The word conversion comes from the Latin *converto*, which means "I turn around." Turning around, turning away from the familiar to the unfamiliar can be rather unnerving at times.

One may be disquieted by what passes for education today without really understanding what education ought to be. Coming to that fuller understanding is a *process*, and in the early stages of that process thinking parents will feel as though their efforts are little more than a farce. Your friends may be asking, "Who do you think you are?" If they are polite enough not to ask in a loud voice, you may still be supplying the question on their behalf.

The only way to answer such questions successfully is through a commitment to hard work over a long period of time. We are tempted to think it would be nice if education could occur on the Big Rock Candy Mountain. But it cannot, and as diligent parents, we are confronted with two areas which stand out with respect to the necessity of hard work.

The first is the necessity of reading, and reading some more. A person can successfully sell someone else on a vacuum cleaner without reading, but he cannot sell someone else on books without reading. *Education is the process of selling someone on books.* Parents who will not read simply cannot be equipped to supply a classical and Christian education for their children. Tragically, even many Christians have been infected with the "affirmative action" approach to learning. We want equal results for unequal effort, but God did not create the world in this way. He is not mocked; unequal efforts will routinely bring us unequal results. This means that we cannot pursue a classical and Christian education as a fad; we are not purchasing intellectual hula hoops for the kids.

While the volume of reading is important, the quality of books read is far more important. Because of this, we conclude many of the sections of this booklet with a suggested reading list for parents. The books suggested will not all be "about" education, but they will all be directly connected to the task of bringing this kind of education to your children. And as you read these books, they will in turn suggest further reading. These lists included here are intended to mark the starting blocks, not the finish line.

The reason we recommend a particular book may not be immediately obvious, and many Christian parents may wonder if some are even worth reading. But for those who undertake the task, the reasons will soon become obvious. Again, the lists are not exhaustive but only a good beginning.

Diligent reading is related to the *second* area where hard work is necessary—that is, in the area of instruction. Children need to be *taught*. Occasionally, a self-motivated and bright child will show the ability to become an *autodidact—i.e.* self-taught. But most children need to be led into an understanding of what they are being taught. The ability to learn on one's own is normally the *result* of a good education, and not normally the *cause* of it. Jesus teaches us that a "disciple is not above his teacher, nor a servant above his master" (Matt. 10:24).

This means that there must be consistent time set aside for instruction in the home, and the parental instructors must be *prepared* to provide that instruction. The reading mentioned above is a significant part of that preparation. Glibness, or an ability to "wing it" is no substitute for reading and study. And while it may be possible to "wow" the younger children, there will come a time when your older children will detect the fraud if you are not prepared. For example, in the area of literature, the students may read and enjoy books that their parents have not read, but they cannot be *taught* literature that their parents have not read. More than this, they cannot be taught literature that their parents have not *studied*.

The last important note is certainly not last in order of importance. The Bible teaches that doctrine—teaching—must be *adorned*. If it is not adorned with a gracious manner and clean-hearted living, the child will likely either come to imitate the hypocrisy of the parents or turn away with disgust from everything given to him, including what was truly valuable. Neither direction is one we should want our children to take. Consequently, the rigor of classical study must not be confused with the rigors of living in an unpleasant home. Consider exhortation from a father in a former century:

> [A child's] character is forming under a principle, not of choice, but of nurture. The spirit of the house is breathed into his nature, day by day. The anger and gentleness, the fretfulness and patience—the appetites, passions, and manners—all the variant moods of feeling exhibited round him, pass into him as impressions, and become seeds of character in him; not because the parents will, but because it must be so, whether they will or not. They propagate their own evil in the child, not by design, but under a law of moral infection.

. . . The spirit of the house is in the members of the children by nurture, not by teaching, not by any attempt to communicate the same, but because it is the air the children breathe. . . . Understand that it is the family spirit, the organic life of the house, the silent power of a domestic godliness, working as it does, unconsciously and with sovereign effect—this it is which forms your children to God.[7]

---

[7] Horace Bushnell, *Christian Nurture* (Cleveland, OH: The Pilgrim Press, 1994, 1861) pp. 36, 119.

Suggested Reading:

The Bible
A Day in Old Rome by William S. Davis
A Day in Old Athens by William S. Davis
The *Iliad* and *Odyssey* by Homer
The *Aeneid* by Virgil
Hamlet, Macbeth, and *Much Ado About Nothing* by
        Shakespeare
Pride and Prejudice by Jane Austen
Holiness by J.C. Ryle
The Rare Jewel of Christian Contentment by Jeremiah
        Burroughs
Fair Sunshine by Jock Purves
Finding the Faith by Douglas Wilson
How to be Free from Bitterness by Jim Wilson
The bi-monthly magazine *Credenda/Agenda*
How to Read a Book by Mortimer Adler
How to Read Slowly by James Sire

A Brief Definition of
Classical and Christian Education

Classical education can best be understood as referring to three rudimentary things. The first has to do with educational method, that is, the pattern of conducting the student through the stages of *grammar*, *dialectic*, and *rhetoric*. Collectively, these three stages have been called the *Trivium*. Although methods of education are not all-important, as some modern pedagogues have assumed, methodology still retains some degree of importance.

The second aspect of classical learning refers to the *content* of the studies, and answers the question, "What subjects are to be studied?" Classical education is distinguished by the presence of subjects like Latin, logic, theology, and rhetoric in the curriculum. At the same time, many of the subjects common to a basic education are also included—history, science, mathematics, *etc.*, omitting classes on Getting In Touch With One's Own Personal Self.

The third aspect recognizes the importance of the historical and cultural position of the teacher and student. Classical and Christian education is indigenous to Western culture; it is the result of Christ being born during the reign of Caesar Augustus and of the earliest missionaries heading west more than they did east or south. Christian parents who seek to impart this heritage to their children are not being xenophobic, or hostile to other cultures. As Christianity permeates the Far East, for example, its cultural impact will certainly be glorious—and quite different from what we have seen in the history of our civilization. But we do not honor another culture by disparaging the achievements of our own culture. Parents who give their children a classical and Christian education are simply recognizing that, in the providence of God, their children have been born into

Western culture; the only choice remaining is whether they will be educated there, in the light of that heritage, poorly or well.

You'll find two other uses of "classical" in the realm of education. For different reasons, evangelical Christians ought to reject both. With regard to the first, the reason for this is obvious. For some, classical means neo-pagan. In the Renaissance, many wanted to return to the paganism of ancient Athens and Rome. But we know from Scripture that the rock of Daniel's vision has struck that particular statue on its feet and destroyed it, and it can never be restored. As Christians we should not *want* it restored, and as creatures, we must be careful not to fight against the decrees of Providence. God destroyed those civilizations, and our duty is to say "Amen" and "Good riddance." We may study the remnants of those cultures with pleasure and profit, but not from any misguided desire to return to those rebellious cultures from which a merciful God delivered us. As Dorothy Sayers pointed out, "Our civilization, such as it is, remains in its living bones a Christian civilization—and the Augustan Latin was never Christian."

Another approach to classical education may be more problematic for some Protestant Christians. This is seen in the rigorous classical study remaining today in some parts of the Roman Catholic church. Of course, the study of Latin is kept alive there, as well as a self-conscious historical and cultural connection with the medieval world. Thomas Aquinas and others brought the ancient philosophy of Aristotle into the modern world, trying to merge it with a Christian worldview. We would go too far afield to address in detail here the reasons for rejecting such an approach, but not least of them is the inseparable connection between Catholic theology, which is certainly unbiblical, and Thomism. Another reason concerns the autonomous use of natural law by Aquinas. In short, the classical Protestant should not be seeking a return to the theology of the medieval scholastics.

This, however, brings a basic question to the front. What *is* meant by a Christian worldview and a Christian education? Christian education is *not* a secular and humanistic education with prayer and Bible class attached to it. Rather, we view the Scriptures as the sole rule of faith and practice. The Bible must be at the center of our thinking. It is not central as a vase of flowers is central to a table—nice, but decorative only—but rather central as an axle is central. Everything in the educational process is to revolve around the revealed Word of God. The Bible, and the Bible alone, occupies this position. As the Reformers put it, in Latin, the language of the Reformation, *tota et sola Scriptura*. Our final allegiance is to *all* of Scripture, and *only* Scripture.

Suggested Reading:

The Bible
The Lost Tools of Learning by Dorothy Sayers
Recovering the Lost Tools of Learning by Douglas Wilson
The Abolition of Man by C.S. Lewis
The Discarded Image by C.S. Lewis
An Experiment in Criticism by C.S. Lewis
The God Who is There by Francis Schaeffer
On Secular Education by R.L. Dabney
Amusing Ourselves to Death by Neil Postman
Christianity and Classical Culture by Charles Cochrane
On Christian Doctrine/Book IV by Augustine
Ideas Have Consequences by Richard Weaver
The Seven Laws of Teaching by John Milton Gregory

Component Parts of a
Classical and Christian Education

The three stages of the *Trivium* are *grammar*, *dialectic* (or logic), and *rhetoric*. In medieval education they supplied the structure for one's general education before proceeding on to what was called the *Quadrivium*.

In the grammar stage, the student learns many particulars, many facts. Note that the word *grammar* here is *not* restricted to language study. Each area of study has a "grammar." The particulars in each subject are many and various. In math, grammar would include division and multiplication tables. In geography, it would include continents, rivers, mountains, and so on. In history, it would include kings, battles, wars, dates, etc. In Latin, it includes case endings, verb endings, and basic vocabulary.

Then follows the dialectic stage, where the student begins examining the relationship between these particulars. What is the relationship between the geography of the East Coast and the first battle of Bull Run? Between Xerxes and Esther? Or, for that matter, between Genesis and the theory of evolution? The student learns about the inter-relatedness of the various subjects he has been learning up this point.

Once the student has learned the basic rudiments, and he has sorted them into piles, the student then learns to express these aquisitions in a more polished way. This is the study of rhetoric.

Now as Dorothy Sayers points out in her seminal essay, "The Lost Tools of Learning," these three aspects of the *Trivium* correspond nicely to three stages of child development. She argues in that essay that our responsibility in education is to "cut with the grain," and require specific things of the students when they are most receptive to them.

She divides children into three groups. The first group

is the youngest, and is characterized by her as the "Poll-parrot" stage. This corresponds generally to younger children, ages five through ten. At this age, children love to chant and memorize, and it is simply foolish not to take full advantage of the opportunity. It is just as agreeable for them to chant *amo, amas, amat* as it is for them to recite *hickory, dickory, dock*. The mastery of the grammar stage requires large amounts of memorization, and Sayers argues that this should be done when memorization is easy and agreeable. Consequently, with the classical approach, the younger children are brought to store away in memory large amounts of information which they do not yet understand. *That* comes at the next stage. Therefore, they memorize presidents, case endings, math tables, spelling words, rivers, and on and on, *ad infinitum*.

The next stage she calls the "Pert" stage. During the junior-high years, children become inquisitive, and they begin to challenge much of what they have been taught, seeking to understand it. There are two errors made at this stage. The first is made by relativistic parents, who let their child question in an open-ended fashion, and who permit the child to question in an autonomous, disrespectful way. But the second mistake is commonly made by Christian parents who feel threatened if a child questions *any* of what he has been taught; they sometimes mistakenly assume that all such questioning must be rebellious.

This pert stage is a golden opportunity to teach the student the laws of logic and proper argumentation. When the child wants to argue, he should be taught proper and responsible argumentation. The study of formal logic should begin at this age (11-13), and the application of it *to all other subjects* should be actively encouraged. At the same time, respect for parental authority must be maintained. Children should not be permitted under any circumstances to pop off. "But Mom, that's the naturalistic fallacy!" There is no better opportunity to teach respect for others than by requiring a diligent and careful analysis of their statements and arguments.

The third stage is the rhetorical stage. In the high-school years, children become more concerned with appearances, and they should be taught how to present themselves well, communicating what they believe in a worthy fashion.

Theology is not excluded from this process. As the queen of the sciences, the Christian worldview is central. For example, in the grammar stage, children memorize verses, books, and basic doctrines of the Bible. In the dialectic stage they learn to think through various problems in the light the Word supplies—"Was it right for the Hebrew midwives to lie to Pharaoh?" In the rhetorical stage, they learn to take what they have learned and present a thoughtful presentation and apology for the Christian faith.

The Basics of Latin

A Case for Teaching Latin

Many reasons commend the study of Latin; we supply just a few of the more basic reasons here.

First, the study of Latin provides an efficient way to learn the grammatical structure of English. As Sayers comments, "English is a highly sophisticated, highly analytical language, whose forms, syntax and construction can be grasped and handled correctly only by a good deal of hard reasoning. . . . To embark on any complex English construction without the Latin Grammar is like trying to find one's way across country without map or signposts."

Second, Latin is a key to about fifty percent of our English vocabulary. Whether such words come to us directly from Latin, or via the Romance languages, many of our words have a Latin source. Understanding the Latin provides the student with many opportunities to enhance his English vocabulary.

In the third place, Latin is the key to all the Romance languages (which are simply great-grandchildren of Latin), and it is indirectly a key to all inflected languages. These Romance languages include Portuguese, Spanish, French, Italian, *etc.* The study of Latin will greatly help the student who goes on to study *any* of these other languages. Latin is a much greater help in the study of Spanish than, say, French is a help in the study of Spanish.

Fourth, the precision of mind required in the study of Latin is a great benefit in other fields requiring such precision—science, for example. The study of Latin requires an attention to detail which, if it has become habitual, can only be a great blessing in other subjects.

Fifth, the literature of western culture is saturated with Latin. As Sayers mentions, "without some knowledge of

Latin it must be very difficult to make anything of it." History, philosophy, law, and literature all require some acquaintance with the Latin language.

In many Christian homeschooling families, the question of Greek study may arise. The study of Greek certainly is valuable, but, other things being equal, it is still our conviction that Latin should take priority. But other things are not always equal. Greek, however, may still win out in the minds of some. Many families want their children to be able to study the New Testament in the original, and far more Christian parents have already studied Greek than Latin. Moreover, because of the connection to the New Testament, far more reference helps are available for Greek. At the same time, Greek *will* remain a harder language for your children to master. But for those parents who are committed to Greek, we would commend the study of Latin as a good platform for the *subsequent* study of Greek. In our own studies, Greek came first, and it would have been easier had it been the other way around.

The Basics of Teaching Latin Pronunciation

Numerous texts and programs are available to aid the homeschooling parent in teaching Latin to the kids. Nearly all of them have some instruction near the beginning concerning the proper pronunciation of Latin, but nearly all are equally unsuccessful in convincing those parents that their pronunciation is adequate. Consequently, some background is in order.

First, you are not teaching *conversational* Latin. Unlike Spanish or French or other modern languages, no culture today speaks Latin. For some this is an argument against teaching Latin at all, and if the purpose of language study were only to aid one in conversations with native speakers, the point would be a good one. But the value of Latin is not found in repartee with ancient Romans. Because this is the case, pronunciation is not nearly as important as it is with modern language study. Mispronouncing Spanish will get you laughed at in Mexico City; the same is not true of "mispronouncing" Latin.

Second, because microphones were not thrust in Augustus Caesar's face, with all his pronouncements duly recorded on tape, we are not exactly sure what his pronunciation was. The educated guesses of classical scholars will show up in texts which follow the "classical" method of pronunciation. This is the school which pronounces *v's* as *w's*, *c's* as always hard like *k*, *etc.* Still, more than a few are not entirely convinced that Latin was really pronounced that way. And, even assuming this pronunciation has been accurately reconstructed, we must recall that it was the pronunciation of the intelligentsia during the brief moments of Augustan glory. We have no transcendent reason why we must endure tremendous turmoil for the sake of maintaining this particular pattern of pronunciation.

This is related to the third point. There are alternative approaches to Latin pronunciation. One approach is the ecclesiastical pronunciation. Some Latin dictionaries will list an ecclesiastical pronunciation key in the front alongside the classical, or antiquarian, pronunciation. The ecclesiastical pronunciation is that used today in the Roman Catholic church, as well as in old Latin hymns, *etc.*

But the third method, simplest of all, is called the "Protestant," "Old," or "English" method. It follows out the bright idea of linking Latin pronunciation to the vernacular. In other words, say it as though it were English.

In all of this, the one thing which is really important about pronunciation is simple consistency, so that a young student is not bewildered or confused. "But I thought you said . . ." In other respects, pronunciation *non est tanti.* It is no big deal. This may upset some classical "purists," but as Dorothy Sayers argued, "The great reproach cast up against

Latin by those who would drive it altogether from the schools is that it is a dead language. But if it is dead today, it is because the Classical Scholars killed it by smothering it with too much love." The greatest value of Latin for most students is indirect, and pronunciation is not really related to such indirect benefits. And for those students who stay with their Latin, most of them will encounter most of it on the printed page. So parents should not worry about it, and, as Sayers advises, "Choose a pronunciation and stick to it."

The Basics of Teaching Latin Grammar

What is said here is presented as a very brief introduction to a few elements of Latin grammar. It may serve the purpose of removing any fear caused by the detailed but intimidating explanations found in the Latin grammars.

The grammatical function of words in English is determined largely by word order. This is not the case for Latin, which is an inflected language. To illustrate, if the words in an English sentence were moved around, "out of order," the result is a complete change in the meaning of the sentence. For example:

> *The boy hit the ball.*
> *The ball hit the boy.*

Here we have the same words, and two completely different concepts. We can take it even further into the realm of nonsense.

> *The the boy ball hit.*

But in Latin, the function of words is determined by the ending placed on the word. For example, the ending -*am* means that a noun is the direct object of the sentence. The ending -*a* means it is the subject, and so forth. Thus:

Puella poetam amat.
   The girl loves the poet.
Poetam puella amat.
   The girl loves the poet.
Amat poetam puella.
   The girl loves the poet.
Amat puella poetam.
   The girl loves the poet.
In order to say that the poet loves the girl we would have to change the endings and say:

Poeta puellam amat.

When young children are memorizing their case endings, they are simply memorizing the various endings that can be placed on the end of a noun—ten for each noun, five singular and five plural. One set of endings is called the First Declension (there are only five declensions) and goes *a, ae, ae, am, a, ae, arum, is, as, is.*

The same sort of thing happens with the verbs, with different endings signaling what person, number, tense, voice, and mood the verb is in. For example, the endings for the present tense, active voice are *o, s, t, mus, tis, nt.* Thus, *amo* means "I love," *amas* means "you love," and *amat* means "he, she, or it loves." Simple, and as my old Latin instructor used to say, "Just like English, only different."

Latin is a very logical language, but the order of the words is not a primary part of that logic. A good program for taking your younger children through the grammar stage of Latin is found in *A Latin Primer, Books I* and *II* by Martha Wilson. Children can happily store away the information found in these books without troubling themselves about what it all means. They are not yet into the questioning, or dialectical, stage. But you, the instructor, are well past that stage and may want to know what it all means. For a good basic introduction, see Doug Wilson's *Latin Grammar*, also put out by Canon Press. For a more detailed grammar, the high school Latin texts put out by Allyn and Bacon are good. The authors are Jenny, Scudder, and Baade.

In the final analysis, learning the grammar of a language is not much good without learning the vocabulary. A good initial goal is to have two to three thousand words memorized within the first two years of study. This seems imposing but it works out to four words a day. This task is made even easier by the fact that many of the common Latin words have made their way into English. It should not be hard to learn the meaning of *frigidus*—cold. Or *femina*, which means woman, or *aqua*—water, and *poeta*—poet.

The Basics of Logic

Logic is concerned with evaluating arguments, and every academic subject involves arguments. Now, of course, in the sense intended here, we are not using the term "argument" to speak of some ugly quarrel between angry persons. In logic, an argument is a *reason* for believing something; an argument is an answer to a "Why?" question. As such, an argument has two important parts: a group of one or more premises and a conclusion. The premises are supposed to be like connected links in a chain from which the conclusion finally hangs. But not just any old connections between the links of the premises and conclusion will hang together properly. Argument links can either be good or bad. Logic is the discipline which shows us how to judge whether an argument is good or bad, whether it fits together properly or not.

We live in a culture which has been politicized and polarized. Consequently, we are tempted to respond favorably to the "applause lines" delivered by people who are on "our side," and to dismiss with contempt those who have said something with which we differ. We may often take sides in such a process, but it cannot be called *thinking*. People can say many true things couched in atrocious arguments, and they construct valid arguments in the cause of error.

As Christians, you want your children to come to the truth, but you must also want them to come through the door, and not as thieves and robbers. It is important to get to the conclusion the right way, as well as getting to the right conclusion. It is not enough to come up with the right answer—a blind squirrel can find a nut every once in a while.

One of the starting points in teaching logic is to enable the student to distinguish between the *structure* or the skeleton or basic framework of an argument and its *content*. The structure of an argument is like a railroad track. It guides the train, the content, along smooth lines. But the two things, the track and the train, are distinct, and each can have its own problems. We can also think of this difference between structure and content as comparable some common procedures in mathematics, especially algebra. In algebra, we can focus on the underlying structure of an equation by using variables that can stand for any numbers whatsoever. On the other hand, we can focus on the more concrete content of an equation by replacing the general variables with specific numbers. We find the same thing in logic, and so we need to get clear on how to evaluate both the structure and the content of an argument.

The primary concern when considering the structure of an argument is *validity*. Validity simply asks whether we have properly obeyed the general rules of argument structure, regardless of the content of the premises. If an argument shows we have not, then it is invalid; if it shows we have, then it is valid. To illustrate, suppose someone maintains that all dogs are Martians, and, that because Fido here is a dog, he must also be a Martian. This content is obviously not true, but the argumentation is valid, since it obeys a rule of logical inference. Validity means that the conclusion is necessarily true *if* the premises are *supposed as true for the sake of argument*. Validity simply seeks to ensure that we have stayed on the railroad tracks, regardless of the contents in the boxcars of our trains.

In a similar way, an invalid argument can be put together with true statements. Suppose someone maintains that Peter was an apostle, and that Abraham Lincoln was a President, and that, therefore, we may safely conclude that grass is green. We should have a problem with this. Everything about this is true except for the word *therefore*. The premises are true, and so is the conclusion, but the argument is poor. It is invalid; it jumps the railroad tracks. So granting that an opponent's argument is merely valid is no great compliment; crazy arguments can be valid. Having a valid argument, then, is only half the work. What we really want is an argument that is valid *and* has true premises—a *sound* argument. And soundness is a much more serious compliment than mere validity. Nonetheless, validity is crucial, and when we fail to make our arguments valid we are guilty of committing a *fallacy of form.*

One of the tools that is used in analyzing arguments is that of substituting symbols for prose. When a student learns how to do this, he is equipped to analyze the structure of an argument at a glance. Suppose someone said that (P) if it rains today, (Q) the farmers will leave the field. They then point out that (Q) the farmers did in fact leave the field, and conclude (P) that it must be raining. This is called the fallacy of affirming the consequent, which can be seen more readily when the argument is placed in symbolic form, where, in this case, capital letters are substituted for statements in the argument (as noted above).

If P, then Q.
Q.
Therefore, P.

Any argument that takes this form is invalid—it does not matter what the statements behind the symbols are. In the same way, any argument which follows the form below is valid.

If P, then Q.
P.
Therefore, Q.

This form is called *modus ponens*, which is Latin for "way of affirming." It is valid regardless of the nouns put in the position of P and Q. If the structure follows this form, then the argument is valid. *Modus ponens* is just one example of a formal rule; there are many others. A good introductory logic textbook will take one through all the formal rules.

So, arguments may go awry by violating a formal rule, such as *modus ponens,* which focuses on the skeleton of an argument or by violating other standards, known as informal rules, which focus on the contents of the premises. Let's turn from briefly considering structure to consider problems in evaluating the contents of an argument.

We generally recognize three main types of *fallacies of content* or informal fallacies, namely, *relevance, inductive,* and *semantic* fallacies. Relevance fallacies are those arguments whose premise contents are irrelevant in supporting the conclusion, though they may appear relevant at first glance. Inductive fallacies are those arguments in which the likelihood of a conclusion is low or lower than intended. Semantic fallacies are arguments whose statements contain unclear terms which interfere with evaluating the argument.

One relevance fallacy is the *abusive ad hominem* fallacy in which one attempts to discredit a person's conclusion by discrediting their person. But someone can have a terrible character and yet have a wonderful argument; the two can be distinct. If the conclusion has nothing to do with the person's character, then discrediting their character is not relevant to the argument. Another fallacy of distraction was labeled by C.S. Lewis as *Bulverism.* This occurs when someone tries to answer an argument by simply explaining and pointing out the motive his opponent had in embracing the argument in the first place, *e.g.* "You are defending infant baptism simply because you admire the Puritans so much." Well, fine. But of course motives are entirely irrelevant to the validity or invalidity of any given argument. Other relevance fallacies include appeals to pity, popular sentiment, pseudoauthorities, etc. A good argument or counter-argument requires that the premises are truly relevant in supporting the conclusion.

One inductive fallacy is represented by another Latin phrase—*post hoc ergo propter hoc*. This means "after this, therefore because of this." It is the mistake of thinking that P caused Q just because P preceded Q in time. It is the mistake made by the man who thinks his shaving in the morning makes the sun rise. Other inductive fallacies include hasty generalizations, slippery slopes, and faulty analogies.

Finally, one semantic fallacy is *equivocation*, in which one shifts the meaning of an expression within an argument. For example, if someone claims that "it is right to allow everyone to take his or her own life, therefore, each of us has a right to his or her own body." Here, the arguer equivocates on two different senses of the word "right," and the argument would fail. Other semantic fallacies include ambiguity, vagueness, and composition.

As mentioned above, the best time to teach logic is during the dialectic stage, which roughly corresponds to the junior-high years. Do not be misled; *average* twelve and thirteen-year olds are fully capable of mastering this material.

Suggested Reading:

Introductory Logic by Douglas Wilson
A Rulebook for Arguments by Anthony Weston
The Art of Reasoning with Symbolic Logic by David Kelley
Introduction to Logic by Leonard Copi
Logic by Gordon Clark
A Concise Logic by William Halverson

The Basics of Rhetoric

The word "rhetoric" has negative connotations for most people. It conjures up images of smooth politicians snowing their audiences with slick euphemisms and patriotic bombast as they attempt to remain in office with ever fatter salaries; of bellowing tyrants fanning huge crowds of mindless followers into a frenzy of genocidal xenophobia; of lugubriously ranting charlatans pacing stages with powerfully modulated semi-melodic syntactical sonorities; of wildly overblown descriptions like these.

That is an image of rhetoric that has plagued it for millennia. The first debate over rhetoric that we know of was between Plato and Aristotle: Plato said that public speakers—orators—were too concerned with style, with superficial flashiness in their words, with persuading audiences by means of fine-sounding eloquence instead of truth and substance. Aristotle agreed that skill in eloquence was often abused, but countered by asserting that the soundest logic is incommunicable without words and that therefore ability in rhetoric is necessary in order to be persuasive. The sophists of the Roman Empire were just that—merely sophists who charged audiences to listen to their highly entertaining speeches—because real political and legal debate was no longer crucial to the state: the emperor had taken over the functions of senate and supreme court. Eloquence got a bad name because of these circus rhetoricians. And yet Augustine argued that preachers should have skill with language in order to communicate spiritual truths to their audiences and to persuade them to obey that truth.

This debate has been repeated, with various changes rung on the same theme, ever since. But the attack is always made with great eloquence, as Plato's was, thus showing that rhetoric is unavoidable; and the answer is always essentially

Aristotle's: communication through language is a characteristic of human beings and therefore we have only two choices—attempt to communicate and persuade by trial and error and accident, or think about what we are doing and try to refine, hone, and improve it.

In fact, Aristotle put rhetoric and logic in the same category. They are both arts of thought and communication that man does by nature, and that therefore must be refined. The rhetorician and the logician are not inventors of rhetoric and logic, any more than a grammarian is an inventor of grammar. They are all engaged in discovering what man does naturally and in cataloguing, categorizing, naming, critiquing, and communicating what they discover so that others may be more efficient in these naturally human arts.

The following basic principles of rhetoric, therefore, are to be considered in that light. They are principles developed in the Greco-Roman world and given renewed vigor in the Renaissance and Reformation; they are principles developed by observation of the way good speakers or writers work. They are not unbreakable rules, but they are steady guides until a student of persuasive communication understands, internalizes, and uses them well and is then able to manipulate ("break") them to his advantage.

Classical rhetoric divided itself into five "canons": 1) inventio, or the stage of developing arguments, illustrations, and substantive content; 2) dispositio, or the stage of arranging that accumulated content into the most advantageous order for persuasive communication; 3) elocutio, or the stage of considering how best to actually say all those things, what words and phrases to use, and what figures of speech; 4) memoria, or committing to memory the completed speech; and 5) pronuntiatio, or effective delivery of the speech. Most modern studies of rhetoric dispense with the last two as being concerned primarily with live oratory and concentrate on the first three as being applicable to a broad range of persuasive communication such as essay, speech, or letter writing, and formal speaking of all kinds.

In the first stage of developing a composition or speech ("inventio"), there are a number of considerations. What appeals will be effective: emotional, ethical, logical? Where logical arguments are used in a particular composition, what kind should they be: comparison/contrast, cause/effect, genus/species, definition? Where emotional appeals are used, how can the audience be moved without being manipulated? And how can the author/speaker impress the audience with his own integrity or credibility so that they will listen to him (the ethical appeal)?

In the "dispositio" stage, a typical order of the parts of a speech have been traditionally followed, though naturally with a great deal of variation. In this generic pattern, the first part, called "exordium," is the introduction. The second, "narratio," is the statement of the thesis or main point of the composition. The third part, called "divisio," outlines for the audience or reader the main divisions, headings, or points to be covered in the composition or speech. The fourth part, "confirmatio," is the actual argument or main discussion of the thesis under consideration; the fifth, "confutatio," is the refutation of possible objections; and sixth, the "conclusio," is the concluding statement, summary, or peroration. This traditional order admits of variation, adaptation, addition, elimination, and recombination of parts, but the essential principles are present in this scheme.

In the "elocutio" stage, the final stage of composition, the author chooses the level of style he will adopt (high, middle, plain), and considers his consistency of style, propriety of style for the occasion, and clarity of expression. He will also consider persuasive language devices such as figures of speech and word choice or diction.

It should be obvious by now that the fundamental principle behind all rhetorical study and practice is that the audience must be considered. Since we communicate not with ourselves but with others, communication involves an audience, whether it is the friend we write to, the congregation we preach to, or the readers we write for. And the audience implies a context and an occasion, both of which must also be taken into account in all the choices made in composition; and the audience either already has formed or will form an opinion of the author/speaker, and that too must be taken into account.

Behind all these principles lies a fundamental learning methodology that has far broader application than just the study of rhetoric. This method turns on the three stages called "art" (or precept), "imitation," and "practice." "Art" means learning the principles of a subject or study. "Imitation" means identifying and copying, in manner and style, and sometimes literally, the best models from the past. "Practice" means exercising oneself constantly in the attempt to incorporate all that has been learned from copying models into an original skill and style of one's own. When the student has diligently studied, copied, and practiced and has begun to internalize the habits of the art of rhetoric, he will discover that rhetoric is more than eloquence; it is a way of gathering, organizing, and using knowledge.

Paul says to the Corinthians that "my speech and my preaching were not with persuasive words of human wisdom, but in demonstration of the Spirit and of power" (I Cor. 2:4), but clearly he uses words and uses them well. His objection is not to the skillful use of words, but to reliance on human persuasion and wisdom; but all gifts and abilities, including those of language, when submitted to the God who gave them become powerful tools for the edification of the saints, the dominion of the earth, and the advancement of the kingdom of God.

Suggested Reading:

Rhetoric by Aristotle
Ad Herennium traditionally, though incorrectly, attributed
    to Cicero
Institutio Oratoria by Quintilian
Lectures in Sacred Rhetoric by R.L. Dabney
Classical Rhetoric for the Modern Student by Edward Corbett
Rhetoric in the Classical Tradition by Winifred Horner
Defense of Classical Rhetoric by Brian Vickers

The Basics of Christian Worldview Thinking

We may conclude from a study of the greatest commandment that one of our central duties is to love God with all our *minds*. Moreover, in Deuteronomy 6:4-9, we are directed to impart the greatest commandment to our children when we get up, when we lie down, and when we walk along the road. In short, we are to be teaching our children this all-encompassing love for God, including an intellectual love for God, all the time.

In order to do this, we must first come to the recognition that God is over all, and in all, and through all. "For of Him and through Him and to Him are all things, to whom be glory forever. Amen" (Rom. 11:36). This recognition that God is sovereign over all things is central to the concept of thinking in a Christian fashion about anything. There is no neutrality in any area of human endeavor because of, and only because of, the sovereignty of God, and of His Son, the Lord Jesus Christ.

This conviction has been given many odious names down through history, but the most popular of such names is "Calvinism." It is important not to be put off by the prejudices generated by name-calling. (Remember the *abusive ad hominem* discussed above!) In order for Christian parents to understand and teach every subject in the light of the Lordship of Jesus Christ, they must first believe there *is* a relationship between Jesus Christ and the subject under consideration. And this is only possible when we understand that God is sovereign over all things.

The task of the Christian parent is to teach his children in such a way that all thoughts are brought under the headship of Christ. "For the weapons of our warfare are not carnal but mighty in God for pulling down strongholds, casting down arguments and every high thing that exalts itself against the knowledge of God, bringing every thought into captivity to the obedience of Christ" (2 Cor. 10:4-5).

We don't bring in this issue for the sake of being "divisive" or theologically cantankerous. It is simply a matter of historical record that the overwhelming number of Christians who have made contributions in the area of worldview thinking have been Christians who have acknowledged and embraced the doctrine of the sovereignty of God. We cannot readily yearn for the fruit but despise the tree it comes from. Given this, it is not surprising that we have so little fruit. Before we can make our way back, a little plain speaking is in order. Unless we recover the full-orbed theology of the Reformation, we will never recover the worldview thinking which is its child.

Fundamental to Christian worldview thinking is the biblical notion of *antithesis.* An antithesis is a sharp juxtaposition of two claims or views. Part of thinking like a Christian means that we aim to rid our outlook of all non-Christian assumptions about the world, history, human nature, knowledge, science, the arts, and every other subject. In its place we seek understanding from God's revelation on each and every concern, for in Christ "are hidden all the treasures of wisdom and knowledge" (Col. 2:3).

To be a Christian is to be in constant, total war. We have no say in the matter, and no one is exempt from serving. This war is not just some sideline feature of the Christian life. It *is* the Christian life. Every step toward seeing "every knee bow" before the Lord of glory is an act of war, whether in faithfulness or hatred. Until that point, the war is ruthless and relentless. The horrific enemy onslaught never ceases.

This war is not only constant but total, unconfined, and overwhelming. It is not limited to the daily fight against our own sin but encompasses everything within and without. It is not limited to our own or any one time but rages in every corner of history. It is not limited to our own flesh-and-blood world and history but is driven by dark clashes in heavenly places.

And as this battle moves us all along, killing and maiming, crushing and roaring, much of contemporary Christianity fights with bumper stickers and self-esteem seminars. As the enemy smiles and schemes to ravage our children and decapitate our churches, we try to play down our differences with our attackers and use their institutions as models for our own. As they mock Christ to His face, we learn to relax, take a joke, and create a more entertaining worship atmosphere. The only thing worse than being cut to death in the middle of a war is having it happen without realizing it.

How do God's people get to this point every so often? We do it by lust. Lust for our own supremacy. Lust for letting our own judgments be true, though God be made a liar. This unfaithfulness, after all, started the war. Our first parents enthroned themselves as judges over God, and we have inherited that family trait. God's enemies revel in the resulting rebellion, never ceasing to try to subvert the King, always denying the reality of the war.

After the initial rebellion, God *imposed* the war between His people and His enemies. It was no accident. The war was decreed. And so the battle has rampaged from Abel and Cain, Israel and Babylon, the apostolic fathers and the Gnostics, the Reformers and Rome to contemporary Christianity and modern egalitarianism.

Since this constant, total war is divinely imposed, we can hope for no peace except on the sovereign King's terms. To lust after peace and compromise in the midst of such a war is the highest form of rebellion. To seek peace and compromise when God calls for war is to seek to deface God Himself.

From Cain to the new intolerance, anti-Christian thinking has schemed to deny the reality of the total war. To admit it, of course, would be to admit sin. So, they must fabricate new fictions to whitewash over the division between the friends and enemies of God. They will insist that we are all one people, one planet, or part of god, not allowing any divisions at all. Or they try to shift the dividing line to that between classes, nations, or races. They will embrace anything as long as they can deny the divinely imposed war, and still fight against the people of God. As Augustine declared so long ago, "To the City of Man belong the enemies of God, . . . so inflamed with hatred against the City of God."

This attempted denial is so powerful and central to the enemy's agenda that they exert every effort to convince God's faithful to agree with them. As angels of light, they sucker the church into pagan attempts to save the earth, tolerate hatred of God, and tone down its "dogmatism" since everything is so fuzzy and unclear anyway. And the people that go whoring after such enticements will meet their just end: "I will return your retaliation upon your own head" (Joel 3:7).

How are we to do battle in this holy war? We ought to repent of our sinful failure to see the total war in its starkest Scriptural truth. We ought to pray for eyes to see through the wicked, yet innocent looking pretenses by which the enemy seeks to devour the Church, from fraudulent environmental values to idolatrous patriotism. *Christians ought to be the most skeptical people on the face of the earth.* We ought, by God's Spirit, to discipline ourselves and our children in the Fruit of the Spirit, the testimony of faithful warfare. And, most assuredly, we ought to live in the unhesitating confidence that Christ has conquered the enemy, "having disarmed principalities and powers, He made a public spectacle of them, triumphing over them in it" (Col. 2:15).

Suggested Reading:

The Bible
Institutes of the Christian Religion by John Calvin
Back to the Basics by Hagopian, Wilson, Jones, and Wagner
The City of God by Augustine
Mere Christianity by C.S. Lewis
The Defense of the Faith by Cornelius Van Til
The Westminster Confession of Faith and *Shorter Catechism*
Chosen by God by R.C. Sproul
Putting Amazing Back Into Grace by Michael Horton
Building a Christian Worldview by W. Andrew Hoffecker
Doctrine of the Knowledge of God by John Frame
A Christian Worldview Declaration by Olasky and
     Schlossberg
War of the Worldviews by Gary DeMar

What General Curriculum to Use

Classical education deals with students as individuals, and it is not bureaucratic in structure. The *desideratum* of such an education is not to produce a "cookie cutter" approach to learning. We don't seek to maintain quality control through some bureaucratic standard of measurement but rather through biblical *wisdom*. High standards in education are always *high*, but they are not always interchangeable, the way GM parts have to be. Two individuals may receive the same instruction, and yet, because of differences in gifts, personality, aptitude, and intelligence, the instruction may result in great differences in the students.

Coupled with all this is the fact that no one publisher "has it all." There is no package deal for classical and Christian education. This means that with many of the subjects you teach, it may be necessary to employ texts which are not "classical" in orientation. This is fine, because in the liberal arts, a tortured attachment to a particular textbook, as though it were the iron ball on the end of the chain, is itself an indication of a nonclassical approach to learning.

This means that your program will be eclectic. You will have to piece it together from various sources. As you do so, you shouldn't be frustrated that your curriculum is incomplete.

In preparation for this overall task, the reading you do should begin with the lists given earlier in this booklet. And we state emphatically, *again*, that the reading of the teacher is more important than the reading of the student. If the teacher reads as he should, the reading of the student will naturally fall into place. But if the teacher is just in search of a "book list" for the student to read, then it is not a classical and Christian education that is in view.

As the task of educating yourself and your children continues and broadens, you will always have a need for more books. And once your reading has begun in earnest, and you have gone down some of the bibliographic trails suggested by that reading, you will soon be in a position to start compiling your own book lists. Nevertheless, a few of our suggestions are listed below. Again, these are in addition to the books listed earlier.

Without question, you will find much in the following reading which you should reject. The point is not to read all these authors with the idea of reconciling or harmonizing what they say. It cannot be done. But as thinking Christians, the fact that we are participating in the "great conversation," as Mortimer Adler put it, does not mean that we agree. As Christians we enter the conversation to present an apology for the Christian faith.

We should remember that with such preparatory reading, a good pace to maintain is to try and finish a book every week or two. This may seem intimidating at first, and if it were considered a hobby, it would be overwhelming. But the task is the education of your children, which is not a hobby but a *vocation*. The word *vocation* comes from the Latin verb *voco*, which means "I call." A person's vocation is his calling; a parent's vocation is to learn in order to teach.

Ancient
The *Bible* should of course be read constantly.
Epic of Gilgamesh
The plays of Aeschylus, Sophocles, Euripides, and
        Aristophanes.
History by Herodotus
The History of the Peloponnesian War by Thucydides
The Lives of the Noble Grecians and Romans by Plutarch

Various dialogues of Plato
Nicomachean Ethics, Rhetoric, and *On Poetics* by Aristotle
On the Nature of Things by Lucretius
The *Annals* and *Histories* of Tacitus
The *Apocrypha*
The *Antiquities of the Jews* and *Wars of the Jews* by Josephus
Metamorphoses by Ovid
Meditations by Marcus Aurelius

Early Christian and Medieval
The *Didache*
On the Incarnation by Athanasius
Letter to the Corinthians by Clement
Consolation of Philosophy by Boethius
The Inferno by Dante
The Prince by Machiavelli
Cur Deus Homo by Anselm
Aquinas: Selected Writings (ed. Robert Goodwin)
The *Koran*
Ecclesiastical History by Eusebius

Modern
Meditations on First Philosophy by Descartes
In Praise of Folly by Erasmus
The Bondage of the Will by Martin Luther
Commentary on Galatians by Martin Luther
Utopia by Thomas More
Pilgrim's Progress by John Bunyan
Dialogues Concerning Natural Religion by David Hume
The Wealth of Nations by Adam Smith
Magnalia Christi Americana by Cotton Mather
Lectures in Sacred Rhetoric by R.L. Dabney
A Defense of Virginia and the South by R.L. Dabney
The Foundations of Social Order by Rushdoony

Historical Theology by William Cunningham
The History of Christian Doctrine by Berkhof
Pilgrim's Regress by C.S. Lewis
Thus Spoke Zarathustra by Friedrich Nietzsche
Idols for Destruction by Schlossberg
Christianity and Liberalism by J. Gresham Machen
Postmodern Times by Edward Veith

Conclusion

Hopefully, this brief overview has supplied homeschool parents new to classical and Christian education a little more grounding in the subject. For those who start walking this sometimes arduous path, the long term blessings for you and your children and their children will far surpass the tangles along the way. So much is at stake. As the great nineteenth-century theologian, R.L. Dabney explained:

> The education of children for God is the most important business done on earth. It is the one business for which the earth exists. To it all politics, all war, all literature, all money-making, ought to be subordinated; and every parent especially ought to feel, every hour of the day, that, next to making his own calling and election sure, this is the end for which he is kept alive by God—this is his task on earth.

We recommend the following resources for further information or books on classical education and/or Christian worldview thinking:

Canon Press
P.O. Box 8741
Moscow, ID 83843
800-488-2034

American Classical League
Miami University
Oxford, OH 45056
513-529-7741

Oxford University Press
200 Madison Ave.
New York, NY 10016
800-451-7556

Greenleaf Press
1570 Old LaGuardo Rd.
Lebanon, TN 37087
615-449-1617

Great Christian Books
P.O. Box 8000
Elkton, MD 21922
410-392-3590

Credenda/Agenda
P.O. Box 8741
Moscow, ID 83843
208-882-7963

Tabletalk
P.O. Box 547500
Orlando, FL 32854
800-435-4343

World
P.O. Box 2330
Asheville, NC 28802
800-951-NEWS